Nude in Winter

nude
in
winter

francine
sterle

TUPELO PRESS

First paperback edition December 2006
Library of Congress Control Number 2006901784

Tupelo Press, Inc.
PO Box 539, Dorset, Vermont 05251
802.366.8185 • Fax 802.362.1883
tupelopress.org

Cover photo by Craig Blacklock from
A Voice Within—The Lake Superior Nudes
By Craig and Honey Blacklock, Jim Brandenburg Blacklock
2004, Blacklock Gallery
blacklockgallery.com
Cover and text designed by William Kuch, WK Graphic Design

Acknowledgments

Special thanks to James Elkins whose scholarship either directly or indirectly
informed many of these poems.

Grateful acknowledgment is made to the editors of the following journals and
anthologies for poems published or forthcoming, sometimes in earlier versions:

Journals:

Bucks County Writer: "The Little Hart"
Crania: "JYM Seated III"
Ekphrasis: "The Batman"
Fieldstone Review: "Self-Portrait"
Pebble Lake Review: "Schiele's Studio, 1909"
Reader Weekly: "Array IV," "On a Painting in Onley's Arctic," "Solitude"
Reflections: "April 19, 1995," Self-Portrait as an Allegory of Painting,"
"Dreaming of Picasso"
Sidewalks: "Peaches," "Gilles' Arm"
Tiferet: "Parable of the Blind," "Untitled: rear view of nude"
Water~Stone: "Two Fox Running"

Anthologies:

33 Minnesota Poets: "Still Life," "Madonna in Prayer"
North Country Sampler: "The Trodden Weed," "Renoir"
Northern Printmakers Anthology: "Before the Caves"
To Sing Along the Way: Minnesota Women Poets from Pre-Territorial
Days to the Present: "Two Fox Running"

For my husband
Jonathan Speare

-III-

-IV-

- I -

Green Violinist
Marc Chagall

He takes a church and paints with a church
He takes a cow and paints with a cow...
He paints with a bull's pizzle
He paints with a Russian village
Paints with a plow
Paints with an angel in the sky

You, sings the violin
You, sings the man with the dark green face

And the dog barks *you*
And a ladder lifts two wooden arms
And a fiddler dressed in purple plays

One foot balanced on a drab brown house
The other anchored to an angular roof

You, sings the violin
You, sings the man with the dark green face

And music blesses the harvest
And music touches each prayer
And his little eden of song
Hums in your blood like a bee.

In the Archivolts at Chartres Cathedral
Left door, Royal Portal

January, two-headed, looks back
      with one face, forward with the other;

March prunes an unruly vine;

May flanks a well-muscled mare,
      a sharp-sighted falcon at rest on his arm;

July, tireless harvester, cuts corn with a sickle;

October knocks down acorns from an oak;

December at long last sits, husband and wife,
      before a festive table, offering
      wine, food, an invitation to prayer.

Drawn to a world that denied
      any trace of drought or death,
doubt or disease, ignored
      the crippling poverty attending this life,
overlooked the oxen's shoulder
      turning red under the lash—

      Go ahead, I said,

      and through that foreign door we slid…

A square room. Surrounded by chalk-white walls
black tables, crates, and chairs, black cushions, black curtains,
the lacquer boxes, black, the ebony glass ash trays,
black vases on black shelves, the Japanese stencil cuts, black,
and Schiele, pious as a monk in a starch-white painter's smock.
Lifting a fine-haired brush eye-level to a stretched canvas,
he revisits his eldest sister's death, father's syphilitic insanity,
this beloved father's agonizing death, his mother's lifelong disapproval,
his fervent, enduring love for his artistic young sister,
revisits the Academy, the disdain, the lopsided morals,
the sumptuous facades, the unnatural obsession surrounding
decorum, decoration, surface. This man on the leash of his senses
waits for Eros and Thanatos to exchange greetings, struggle, refuse
to step out of each other's way, and with rapid strokes, draws his own
ghostly body, half-clothed, tattooed to reveal the edges, the angularity,
no points of reference except his own disarticulated body,
the exposure so complete he fixates on the divided self
distended against a blank backdrop, on his long-standing mirror
tilted to take in a look of hunger that will never let him go.

Self-Portrait
Toulouse-Lautrec

I disappear into the streets with my wide behind
and a nose like a potato. Only in Montmartre's
dance halls and dens does no one notice
a dwarf with drooling lips and a lisp.
Walking these rat-infested streets all night,
night after night, I drag my friends from the cabarets
to the circus to the cafés, move from light to light,
port to brandy, gin to vermouth.
It's in the brothels that I feel at home.
8 Rue d'Amboise. 24 Rue des Moulins.
The *égout des spermes*. Outcasts like myself.
Black-stockinged legs. Mouths red as a drip of blood.
Ingres believed the only way to possess a woman
was to paint her, and I want to paint every woman I see.
Look at them: naked and stretched out like animals.
They admit me everywhere and at any moment.
I watch them dressing or touching or taking a bath.
I'm a coffee pot with a big spout.
I'm digging my grave with my cock.
Degas thinks my work stinks of the pox,
but I draw what I see: a woman making a bed
or brushing her hair, someone talking in the salon,
playing cards, humming a song.
When they lie down together, you've never seen
such tenderness. They're like two birds
burying themselves in each others' feathers.
No one will ever love me like that.

Man and Woman
Max Beckmann

Mercurius has come to Eden.
Mercurius, whose mind is quicksilver,
fashions a desert until once holy ground
looks parched, shriveled, sick,
until there's a new Paradise
transformed into a forked stick,
into the stunted limbs of a plant
topped by milky flowers,
into this man, back turned,
so his muscled flesh
suggests what isn't seen,
what is withheld, what a man can do
in willful blindness to this woman
ribboned on hot sand
like a sunning snake, exposed,
for everyone to see.
Sealed off but bound by proximity,
they do not speak, do not exchange
the simplest of glances.
The hurled words behind them,
they've perfected whole years like this one.
In the thirsty air, on this naked
raft of land, there is no turn toward tenderness.
What's left of affection shimmers like a mirage.

Saints for Sale
Berenice Abbott

If you regard miracle workers as the Lord's
imitators, if you admire their solemn devotion,
if, by proclaiming their heroic virtues, you praise
their fidelity to God's grace, if you believe
these canonized few do intercede on your behalf,
if their holiness sustains your hope as a follower,
and if, by the example of their charitable lives,
you vow to continue the work of salvation,
to praise and be witness of those who live
lives in exalted service to God's plan,
look no further for the pure of heart:
Castitas, Virginitas: women on pedestals,
cradling Christ, hands folded in prayer
or kneeling, heads bowed, unadorned and standing
there in the storefront and offered for sale, an entire
communion of saints, their convincing army ready—
Sancta sanctis!—to prove what they're worth.

Do you believe in the bat?
    I believe in the bat.

Do you believe in the bat and the man?
    I believe in the man.

The man and his corroded wings?
    Wings rise with every beat.

I believe in the otherworldly sounds.
    And I believe in the hovering.

But what of the ambivalence?
    It's difficult to choose between.

And the first sign of erasure?
    Something eaten away.

Something eaten away in an act of faith.
    A spectral education.

Do you believe in the angels?
    I believe in the angels and their enduring lives.

Do you believe in the cave?
    And the sleeping creatures within.

Think of ten thousand clinging to that wall.
    And the bell-like notes of their breathing.

Do you believe darkness embeds itself in the soul?
  I believe in the soul.

So this is our savior?
  As surely as it is about being saved.

The body's a cobweb.
  Into the holes air will dip its hands.

I have very little of Mr. Blake's company;
he is always in Paradise.
—Catherine Blake

"Christ…is the only God…
and so am I
and so are you."

Albion rose from where he labored at the Mill with Slaves…

Beneath his feet,
a writhing worm,
a bat-winged moth:

creatures of darkness,
dispelled by Blake
in his cramped rooms

wearing threadbare trousers
caked with inks and wax,
by divine creation

wreathed in shining light.
Behold: the compassed self
splay-legged, arms outstretched,

burnished gold
haloed around him,
his nakedness

more radiant than the sun.
No pumps or pounding pistons.
A look of exultation on his face.

Harmony
Remedios Varo

The medieval mood. The monklike cell.
The monklike mood in the medieval cell.

In there in there in the chair in there in the chair's
split upholstery chair an egg-filled nest
nesting in the split-open chair.

And a motherbird arriving. One bird again and again
and the arriving.
Again a motherbird arriving again and again the.

Pushing up tiles up flowers and trees pushing the tiles
pushed up by flowers pushing and the pushed up trees.

Wisps of ethereal matter escape from a parquetry floor.
Little ghostlike. Little *trompe l'oeil* illusion.

Skewering jewels and geometric solids on a staff of metal threads
she's unaware of the apparition on the wall
mimicking her movements or the apparition on the opposite wall
mirroring the mimicking of a saintly woman and her muse
making music out of air.

Take in the glass bottles the books the wide-open chest
the desk the clerestory windows the vases of glass
the rope ladder going past the books to the bed.
A ladder is not a door. A desk is not a piano.

Within arches within ogival arches within that architecture
meant to define and align with harmony and devotion confined
within these arches see harmony and devotion refined.

Madonna in Prayer
Giovanni Battista Salvi da Sassaferrato

Because it is the cloth of grief
Because it covers her with light
    as if it were a garment
Because the threads of it build a bridge
    across temptation
Because its robe is woven into every mother's cry
Because it allows her to wear
    hope's colors in her hair
Because it swaddles her as a blanket swaddles a baby
Because it binds faith to affliction
Because it knows she is frail
    and its mercy cloaks her
Because it is the braid of fear
    the ribbons of thanksgiving
Because it is a precious lace she makes
    with her neediness and longing
Because belief need not precede it
Because doubt will not diminish it
Because it is the green shawl of the forest
    the delicate gown of a flower
Because it opens the seam of the heart
    and ties her to the divine

Teach me to wear her grace like a coat
Teach me to quiet my thoughts and speak
Teach me to silence my words and listen

Peaches
Claude Monet

> *Only an eye but God what an eye...*
> —Cézanne on Monet

One learns to recognize the grove's green
sound in the leaves, but there's more to it,

more than light flung down on a table
across a spill of fruit, more than learning to see

immortality or *abundance* on their fair red cheeks.
Peaches of the mind. The weight of them.

Ripened in summer sun. Touched by the erotic.
What a fire he's made, capturing the moment

dull oil paste turns into luminous fruit
as he says what's unsayable, says it

with a scruffy mess of glints and tangles,
brushstrokes that lift and swivel, twist and turn,

says it over and over again until painter and painted are one
and the fruit's sweet flesh comes alive in your hand.

Two Fox Running
Sterling Rathsack

Who lives on the forest border.
Who crawls from a cave beneath the roots of a stump, crawls
from the sandy apron of soil spilling from his den.

Who bats at beetles and butterflies until one day,
launching into an arcing leap,
lands forepaws first on a startled vole.

Who can be coaxed out of hiding
by kissing the back of your hand,
mimicking the sounds of a squealing rodent,

but who vanishes amid dense scrub-growth,
blends to his surroundings, moving
the way the wind moves through a field of wheat.

Whose soft yap chases meadow mice into the leaves.
Whose tracks form a perfectly dotted line.
Whose tracks follow the railroad's punctuated ties.

Who is deliberate in his movements.
Who does not know the agility of his track.
Who does not complicate the world with these abstractions.

Whose steady eye stalks song birds and ground squirrels.
Who does not apologize for his cunning.
Whose every sense wakens in the chirping air.

Fox whose tail is russet red.
Whose tail is a brushfire.
Whose burning tail flashes in flight.

- II -

Please Touch

Marcel Duchamp: Cover for the deluxe edition of the catalogue
for *Le Surréalisme en 1947*

A black velvet backdrop.
A hand-painted, foam-rubber breast.

It's an invitation.
Her nipple is a door bell.

Plump as a raspberry,
It welcomes you in.

Consider the appeal:

The lush body. Pouting lips.
Touch. Please touch.

Not a hint of delay in her voice.
Not a moment's deferral.

It's expectancy mixed with reverie.
The salvation of the erotic.

Instinct is everything.
It fills (whatever's missing) in.

Satyr and Maenad

Fresco in the Fourth Style, House of the Epigrams, Pompeii

aroused   repeatedly aroused
stub-footed   goat-eared   seated Satyr

embracing a kneeling Maenad
her pale skin   broad bottom   hedonic
votary of fertility   vegetation in her hair

there's no sign of the wine   the animal skins
the *thyrsi*   there's no frenzy to these revelers

where's the verdant mountainside   the orgiastic rites
the stupor for the ambrosia-mad   where
the suckled kids and fawns torn apart with bare hands

they'd have devoured the god   communed with him
not stopped until the archaic peaks were numb with blood

between ecstasy and terror   heaven and hell
they of the senseless nights   they of the rioting
they bid you sing   dance   they bid you be merry

A red cock crows
three times at the window
as if something important
had been held back all night,
and now, with the first
crack of sun on the barn,
he unsilences the world.

꙳

Hidden in the treasury of the Vatican,
a rooster's bronze sculpture: its head,
a penis, rests on the torso of a man.
Inscribed on the base of the pedestal,
these words: *Saviour of the World.*

꙳

St. Peter flaps his wings in the dust,
pecks dry corn, thrashes
into a white clump of chickens.
He has announced the day,
and he is hungry.
Scratching at the grain,
his wattles—red as fire,
red as the drop of blood
he left in the brooder—
swing back and forth.

꙳

Love, do not go near him.

☙

A cradling sleep
broken again by cock cries.
Even in dreams
you see him on the weathervane,
hear him cry from the cathedral.
His voice spreads out, empties
out of him as he stands erect
proclaiming the night of darkness
over, insisting that light has come
because of the vigil he keeps
day after day, century after century.

☙

After the strutting cock crows,
after the flaming cock
heralds the day, your head
rings with his echo,
and your own cries burst forth
from the gates of sleep
as you wake to watch
the sun, hour by hour,
in the red heat of the day.

J.Y.M. Seated III
Frank Auerbach

Rubbed back to the whites,
to the pale grays, her head's
been erased, replaced by another
tilting left, leaning the way
the chair leans in ashen space.
Eyes open upwards to the right,
two smears matching the charcoal
slash of her mouth, the coffin-black
hole of her nose. What's left
cannot resist the repeated rubbing
and erasure. How easily an arm
blurs or a breast. How easily
she loosens to fill the chair's
tarry light. Lost in thought,
does she have a thought that
hasn't quite found form? A three-
dimensional word rests on her tongue.
How many tries did it take to make
that tentative thought unthinkable?

The Guitar Lesson
Balthus

This lesson is black and white—
the zebra-striped keyboard,
the checkerboard frock,
the teacher's black velvet shoes
paired with the schoolgirl's
immaculate socks—
but it requires interruption.
The dwarfed guitar must be tossed aside.
This lesson thrives on opposition:
a woman braced in a chair,
a swooning child, naked from thigh to navel,
draped in her lap. With a determined hand,
the music teacher yanks back her pupil's
streaming hair, and the spellbound girl—
legs outspread, her bulging vulva
engorged with blood—is held in thrall.
Look at how her slender arm hangs down
languid as the Pietà, how her eyes
flutter closed till she's suspended
between this world and the next,
how her left hand clings to her teacher's
drab gray dress to expose a breast.
Dazed to the point of dissociation,
knees scab red as if she's been forced
to kneel on the hardwood floor, her body
will do what it's been taught to do.
One cruel lesson can define a life.

Hans Bellmer's Doll

He wanted to be buried with her,
a girl smelling of glue
and wet plaster, with hollow legs
encased in hard plastic shells,
with a recycled head and hands;
a girl with two arms, four legs,
four decorous breasts, with
three pelvises and an upper torso
above a spherical belly; a girl with eyes
like marbles and a scrappy black toupee,
with a satin bow and a couple of wigs;
a homemade model with moveable ball joints
who wore long hose, white anklets,
a schoolgirl's woolen beret,
and black Mary Janes; this girl
with a multiplication of parts
could be bound with twine,
tied to a tree, hung on a hook, pulled
apart, limbs strewn down the stairs,
could be dismembered
piece by piece, given a Siamese
twinlike arrangement of four legs
and two hairless pelvises around
the central ball of her stomach,
eliminating the torso, arms, and head.
The girl he photographed
hundreds of times
in hundreds of menacing positions
was to lie with him
as the dust of eternity settled on those
rosy bruises he'd painted on her legs.

Jan van Riemsdyck's *Drawing for Tabula XXVI* in William Hunter's *Anatomy of the Human Gravid Uterus*, 1774, a British Obstetrical Atlas

Fire-colored chalk signals
depth and volume,
organs, fat, flesh,
even light as it glances off
the torso's torn-open cavity,
as it is slowly absorbed by
softly-wrapped, wax-injected thighs.
Buried face down in bulging intestines,
her decapitated skull
teeming with wormy fissures
suggests a fetal world seething below.
Leathery flaps of skin, folded back,
hide the breasts while her womb
pulled back and pale as clay—
this woman died before giving birth—
is accented by a rim of curling,
rust-red pubic hair.
The vaginal opening is screened
by an open book whose patterned spine
binds the fanlike gills of its pages.
So, *this,* these men tell us
is where science and art begin...
                    and so we stare
at her mutilated body,
her dismembered limbs highlighted
by those sensual veils of cloth,
that hairless head composed
to look like a swelling belly,
but the bodiless self is suppressed,

the one, no doubt, with a name
and a voice and a family, the one
chilled by illness, by the thought
death would come first to her
then to her unborn baby, a woman
too poor to escape the same fate
as the bloody-headed Gorgon.

Dalí's Edibles

Do you have a stomach for viscera,
marrow bones, shreds of flesh,
tolerance for severed limbs,
intestinal pulp, appreciation
for oral delirium and the belief that
Man's most philosophical organs
are his jaws? How about an appetite
for runny, intrauterine eggs
or the loaves of surrealist bread
he sucked and softened and kneaded
on a table? Do you want to see
the butchery of tunny fishing,
the bloody sea water no bullfight
ever matched? In exploring your own
labyrinthine unconscious, have you ever
balanced grilled lamb chops on a lover's
bare shoulders or been distracted
by the erotic mobility of spoons,
the evocative shape of a fork or craved
the savory brain beneath a bird's bony skull?
Have you ever been or will you ever be
obsessed with shellfish? If looking
at a picture is eating, are you sated
by those molecular models of grapes?
Does carnality make you salivate?

Ophelia
Antoine Préault

In a spool of water,
she has gone mad.
Death is one wave,
betrayal, another.

It doesn't take much to complicate a life.

Her delicate neck,
lithe as marshgrass,
bends to the current.
The mind lets loose its fury
as river water swirls
over the spurned earth.

Lilith

Kiki Smith

She of the night.
Mud-brown bronze.
Succubus with glass eyes,
she crouches…
not out of lust or fear but out
of torment.
Banished to the void
  for disobeying Yahweh
    refusing Adam's orders
      ignoring the three angels
whose dead script fell on deaf ears:
imagine the implications,
the shadow she would cast.
Lilitu, storm-harlot, owl-hag,
Goddess of desolation.
From the windy hell of revenge she flies
fast as a bat from its cassock-black cave
to swoop down on men as they sleep,
drain semen from men as they sleep.
Night monster, she-demon, nocturnal maid.
She will do anything to make herself known.
Winged and wild-haired, she seeks
churchmen who judge her to be
polluted, dangerous, unclean.

The Little Hart
Frida Kahlo

After nine downturned arrows
pierce the hart's warm hide
one arrow for each muse
one for each of the nine heavens
the nine plains of hell the nine
gods of darkness the nine stages
through which the soul passes
to find rest the nine months
the children she'd miscarried
needed but never had

She stands alone on the forest floor
stunned by the blood by the penetration
the arrow's aim the force of its
impact the strength of whoever it was
drew the bow time and time again

She stands resigned
once again to her fate to the torment
which will not be assuaged
the disfiguring plaster jackets
the repeated surgeries the confinements
the husband's affairs O slaughtered stag
with lyre-shaped antlers O tree of life

Shorn to a single green bough
and laid at her feet

Self-Portrait as an Allegory of Painting
Artemisia Gentileschi

A woman in a man's world, a woman
making a claim, choosing her own body
as the source of inspiration, wearing, as Pittura did,
a gold chain bearing the mask of imitation:
her tousled hair and muscled arms,
the shifting gold-green colors of her dress,
her sleeve rolled to the elbow,
the light striking her brow and the shadow
made by the mask-shaped charm against flesh,
the double mirrors she used to paint herself,
the act of it captured mid-gesture,
the paints laid out as her father taught her:
white near the thumb then red, brown, green,
her well-curved body bending around the canvas,
the calculated self-image occupying
the full height of the picture, her unromanticized face,
dramatically lit, composed, the bare bodice,
the rolled-up sleeve, her eyes turned upward,
her right arm raised, its movement frozen,
the mind in motion, her wide, searching gaze.

You Cannot Step Twice into the Same Stream
On a Painting by Eleanor Bishop Speare

Dropping   in a dimpled stream
not three   lead sinkers
carrying   a glistening fishhook
to the   untamed river bottom
but   what Heraclitus thought
as his words   snag on a fallen branch,
twirl   midstream in the
tea-colored   water. This
is why I've come: to fish
the river's   shifting lines,
to fish   the depths of it, to see
patterns   atop stark bald rocks
jutting   near the shore and read
the story of   the uncounted
years it took   to cut away
a point or   straighten a bend
as water   finds its way around
every obstacle.   *You cannot*
step twice into   the same stream.
Running water is   fluid form
like blood or sap   or semen
but exposed: bugs skim it,
deer drink from it,   turtles burrow
in its muddy ooze.   I've seen
how a river   cuts through
a weightless   wave of wildflowers
nodding   along the bank,
how   migrating geese steer it
in the right   direction, how
an upland basin   overflows,

trickles downhill,   cuts open
a channel, tearing   rocks and roots
and wet-footed weeds   loose from the banks,
how the backwaters   roar with snowmelt
and the half-drowned   cottonwoods
shake sideways   against the flow
and how, when a   red-tailed hawk
circles above it,   a planet is born.
The river moves   like a woman
who has laid down   her hair in the water.
Her breathing   floats to my ear.
Out of nowhere,   a cry of envy from the crow.

Dancer with Red Stockings
Edgar Degas

One's no more than a ghost,
a shivering girl half-glimpsed
and seated beside another
dressing to leave,
wearing a puffed tutu
in hatched strokes of black,
a fanfare of stockings,
vibrant in this cheerless room,
and satin shoes on her weary
dancer's feet held in place by silk cords
twined around her ankles.
Coarsened by years of exercise,
the dancers—one, flesh and blood,
the other, lapsed into thoughtful
incompletion—have limbered at the barre:
jetés, pirouettes, fouettés,
assemblées, petit temps, battements.
No longer defined by an illusory
pool of limelight, they sit stoop-shouldered
in an unplanned pose. The girl's torso,
charcoal mixed with blue pastel,
sets off a splash of scarlet on her lips,
the dense red siren of her legs.
Tomorrow is Sunday.
She will walk through the garden.
She will lie back in her chair.

Nude in Winter

Photographer: Craig Blacklock
Model: Honey Blacklock

This is a story
about the self,
the body guarded
by thick tusks of ice:
glistening knife tips,
the ogre's dripping teeth.
The naked body
tells a story
about frozen space
and the vertical hours
that run on
endlessly,
about the soul
entombed in ice,
about the blameless
cage of the mind,
each thought cold
and clear and sharpened
by constraint, about desire,
how it melts what it touches,
and the unexpected
pivot of energy
when the sleeping body
is about to wake,
when the polished river of the body
is about to wake, when ice
weakens at the edges,
creaks and strains, shudders
and cracks and in one
godlike roar breaks

apart till great blocks
                float free, collide
                        and shatter and over-
turn, floes piling up, ice
                screeching, the grinding
                        ice careening downstream,
slamming into banks,
                uprooting trees, shearing off
                        bare branches, stripping
bark as it's swept along,
                as water is unleashed,
                        as water fills the mouth,
spills from the eyes, flows
                like milk from a breast,
                        water gushing back to earth,
feeding the soil, feeding
                the black seed until it
                        explodes into green and
bursts forth into the world
                with its dignity and power
                        and its brutal beauty.

-III-

The Trodden Weed
Andrew Wyeth

How long to paint the fawn-colored field,
the dying blades of grass,
     building up the ground
         stroke by stroke to make it flow
           forward toward the viewer;
how long, the spiral weed trod underfoot?

With a tempera panel placed flat on his lap,
     his arm supported in a sling
         suspended from the ceiling with pulleys
           and iron weights, he insisted:
To hell with the arm. I want to paint this picture.

This is the high ridge he hiked to regain his strength.
Those are the thigh-length
     French cavalier boots he wore
         (once owned by his father and before that
           by the man who taught his father to paint).

Above his clumsy, leather-clad legs,
the flowing black bottom of a coat
     as foreboding as the fur-coated figure of Dürer
         who visited him in a vision,
           who held out his hand
as Wyeth lay unconscious on the operating table:

his chest split top to bottom,
the shoulder muscles severed to remove
     a diseased lobe in his lung. As he lay there
         addled by the sleep of anesthesia, believing

his boyhood idol had come to take him away,
his heart nearly failed under the strain of it.
The next day, a second brush with death.

So it loomed as a man who will arrive.
So it sank like a heart into the trampled weed.
The land goes brown that once was green.
And life is lived one foot to the other.

Serenity that only instinct can provide.
Charm, impulse, sensuality: the world
all dappled light and pretty flesh: the subtle
tilt of a head, the tender tipping of a foot.
Everything lush, mature, romantic.
Consider the pale-primed canvas,
the flake-white undercoating
thinned by linseed oil and turpentine.
And color, a strong, bright palette.
I want red to sing out like a bell.
Small dabs across the surface of a face.
A feathery, delicate touch in ivory black,
cobalt blue, raw sienna. A sunny world.
An uncomplicated attitude
toward that chorus of lumpy, luminous women.
Even in the end, although crippled by arthritis,
weakened by bronchitis, paralyzed in his legs,
an invalid in a chair who could not prepare
his colors, could not pick up a brush,
who had to have it tied in his hand with a rag,
Renoir painted, experimenting with flattened
perspectives, a simplified color range, softer,
more expressive brushstrokes. Even in the end.
The body is entitled to some lyricism.
I want to say this in front of everyone.
The body is entitled.

Pink Angels
Willem de Kooning

Not quite recognizable, but for everyone these angels:
    a scaffolding of: legs here   buttocks
there   angular eyes   a swooping arm
opera pink   livid pink   pink of the flesh
               non-corporeal beings
tension   between flatness &   the illusion of depth
Angel is the name of their office, not their nature
St. Michael   St. Gabriel   St. Raphael
    guardian angels   who closed the earthly paradise
     protected Lot   stayed Abraham's hand
oblique lives   shell-pink features materializing   less legible than
Supplices te rogamus...
        In Paradisum deducant te angeli...
figure and field merge the world flattens compresses
scale shifts   elegant ovoid forms   form overlapping
                              form
and the motif of the rectangle:
     shocking pink window frame   in
        the shallow space of the picture plane
angels loosened from their bodies, whose power is?

Man Pushing Door
Jean Ipousteguy

Look at me—

eyes round as ball bearings,
    rough back, muscled thigh,
a leg stepping through
        the closed, louvered door,
my expressionless face,
      robotic head,
that determined hand breaking
        through the smoothly finished door
and the other one, mismatched
        and disconnected from my body.

That's not what I want remembered.
    How I want to be remembered.

Not the mechanical mask I wear,
the boundary I defy,
the patchiness of being human.
Not what erupts, protrudes, goes through.
Not the heaviness of that washboard door.

I walked away from my life.
    Got stuck as I was walking.
A thought can petrify like a rock.
    Now I cannot move. Cannot move.
Cannot.

When the Statue Arrived

At first they were overjoyed:
The beautiful marble boy,
His extended hand
Ending in the sun's rays.

They ran their fingers over him.
His classical nose,
His smooth, smooth cheek.
He was theirs, and he was perfect.

Not a single line on his face.
How they cherished him
And his chiseled heart.
But over time he changed.

First a little hair on his cheek.
Then the hand, closing.
The smell of a gun.
His cold, fixed stare.

Once war broke out,
He vanished with the others.
At night they dreamed of him—
Stiff, silent, utterly alone.

When they saw him again—
The bandages off,
Both arms gone,
The pedestal missing—

He gazed vacantly into space,
The broken pieces
Spread out around him.
Draped in a hospital gown

Thin as a cafeteria napkin,
The wounded boy didn't say a thing.
At four in the morning, after limping
Down the melancholy corridor,

He walked straight out the door,
Took a wet step through the snow
And then there was sinking
And then, a shivering wind in his face.

The Hand of Death
Käthe Kollwitz

Life adds on a piece at a time
until one day you're stoop-shouldered:

each labored breath tightens in your chest.
Like an icy branch of winter air,

a clear idea reaches out to you.
It is a simple kindness you accept.

Head bowed like last summer's peonies,
you are simply too weary to refuse.

Someone has come to greet you.
Someone has come to take you in hand.

Gilles' Arm
Nan Goldin

Confined for weeks.
It's a kind of exile.
A glass of water
by the sickbed.
Where is the bread?

❧

In a ledger his lover
keeps track of pills
the doctors prescribe.
He hears there's another
poison they want to try.
He swallows, then picks up a pen.

❧

His ruby blood
pulses toward the needle's heat.
How precious it looks
as they drain it—
color of a king—
a test tube at a time.

❧

Custard and melon and milk,
gravy on a slab of kidney-colored meat.
A lump of it hits the floor:
the same thump a bird
makes against the window in a storm.

⚜

After the chaplain's visit,
he sees a scepter-like lily
dangling from the doctor's
benevolent mouth as if he
were Christ, as if he were
the savior of the world.

⚜

He sleeps fitfully,
snores like a foghorn.
Harbor,
Safe Harbor.

⚜

Talk turns to his father.
Pain's heartbeat
in the flung words,
the forced smile,
his hollow stare.

⚜

He's lost five, maybe ten
pounds in a month, month
after month. His shaved head,
exaggerated as a Titan's,
cannot lift itself from the bed.
Today is his birthday.
It's a simple celebration:
a half-opened bar of chocolate
and apple juice in a plastic cup.

No one hears his last breath,
a clear note
across the chord of his life.
He lies on starch-white bedsheets,
his outstretched arm
thin as tinder.

Still Life

On the immaculate cloth, an arrangement:
a bowl of lemons, a wedge of brie,
a pitcher of red wine, a cut-glass vase
filled with orange and yellow sweetly-
budding mums. *Natures mortes.*
It's a morgue housed in the hospital basement
with its creased paper sheet
draped over a stainless steel table
where a fresh corpse has been
laid out with his rosy head,
sponged genitals, fatty,
waxen thighs, a tuck of string
around his tagged big toe.
I will never love the polite lines
and dead air framing those lavish
portraits of fruit,
the richly textured plates and glasses,
that sickly whiff of flowers.

Buttoned-down Landscape
Dorothy Hall

Buttons harbor in the heart
like pebbles left on a tombstone
marking visits to the dead.
When the world falls away,
the geology of grief presents itself:
a torn strip of black lace,
and on flanks of crumbling dirt,
gashed glass, a metal tag
covered in esoteric code,
a gilt-thin window
lifting off like a wingbeat.

Earth's an interior composition
at the mercy of time, water, the pressure
of concealment, deforming forces
folding and cementing, the unrelenting
compacting of mud, rock, clay,
the colors of sunset materializing
in the whorled heat where eras
and epochs map the shifting deposits,
the unexpected upheavals.

Following the faultlines underground
past layers of limestone, sheets of slate,
past hidden periods of anguish and anger
to the buried veins of regret,
the unconformities, the intervals of erosion,
memory leafs out like the tree
I planted for my father when I was seven,
the rootball's tangled cocoon
now spilling through the soil.

April 19, 1995

Does it hurt?
Let it...
—Vladimir Mayakovsky, "Hope"

Goya would have known what to do
with those circles—blue ones
marking bits of suspicious debris, pink ones,
body parts that were blown blocks away.
Goya would have ignored traditional
composition and plotted lines of force,
dispensed with axes and centerpoints,
and splashed down color in a frenzy
to picture the nesting house sparrow
mashed into chicken wire or sketched
the shredded flag and plastic playthings
tangled around blasted pipes, loose wires,
random shoes, and with a furious hand
fleshed out a woman with her leg slashed
almost in half, an eye lens punctured by glass,
one ear dangling from a gash in her scalp.
On a canvas pale as the plains of Oklahoma,
Goya would have painted the man
stumbling from the blasted building,
a sheet of glass sticking from his back
like a ghastly wing and a dark red jet
spurting from an artery in his neck.
Goya would embrace this scene.
These people. With unrelenting strokes,
he would paint the brief colors of spring
delicately wakened in the funeral flowers
stuffed into holes of a chain-link fence

then lead us to the woman's skull found
crushed beneath a concrete slab, to the legs,
charred almost beyond recognition, half-buried
beneath a pile of crumbling plaster and steel shelving.
In blazing colors smeared on with a palette knife,
we would see the crumpled cars burning
in the distance, and the trained dogs circling,
disoriented by the overpowering odor of death.
As his strokes grew more and more agitated,
as the planes dropped violently away,
as Goya threw down clots of pigments
and added acid touches to the mangled
debris swirling across the canvas,
our eyes would follow as he led us
through ten tons of rubble to find a woman,
breathing, a doctor lying on top of her,
blood from a body above dripping on his brow
as he severs her leg without proper anesthetic.
In an exaggerated clarity of vision,
the unsheltered world would explode,
and in the midst of fire and flying glass,
in the midst of Goya's fiercely balanced lines,
we would be forced to see the children's bodies
counted and carried off, like soldiers
so cold and pale and empty-eyed
scattered across a battlefield's black grass.

Parable of the Blind
Pieter Bruegel

About the death of the eye.
About disjunction, inner and outer, an abyss of darkness.
About deliverance from death: *vivas in Domino.*
Deliverance from misery: *in pace.*
About the old seer's outstretched hand,
the tilted heads, the exaggerated eye sockets.
About the rags on their bodies
and the staves that guide their steps.
About the world we cannot see,
the unseen world which encircles us.
About the words we use: *deprived, benighted, obscured.*
About the mystery of wickedness,
the stooped beggar, the struggling cripple.
About the biblical narratives: Samson, Isaac, Zedekiah.
The mythic blind: Oedipus, Polyphemus, Polymestor.
About the one prostrate in the ditch
and the one behind him, doomed,
and the ones after that, all doomed.
About history, transgression, sacrilege.
About the Syns of vision.
Walkers in strainge Landes.
About what waits in the thickets
and the fall, the inevitable, stumbling fall.
About Unbeleefe
and the invisibility of the divine.
About adversity in a pathless world.
About ignorance.
About infirmity.
About what awaits you
who think you can get through hell in a hurry.

The Yellow Christ
Paul Gauguin

As one begs for mercy, as You
to God in the garden, as white-hatted
peasant women who kneel at Your feet,
as one who has begged…

            Who is the man
with his leg over the wall?
He's all in black and turning
away from the sallow body
searing the eye like a sun,
away from the wood of the cross,
though it's the only ladder
by which to get to heaven,
away from the crown of thorns,
the rope, club, tapered sword, away
from the lance and the sponge,
the column with cord, the scourge.

Before death the skin goes yellow.
Even the sulphurous fields
bounded by a yarn's width of water,
by the tree's harmless flames
cannot escape the pierced palms,
the jaundiced air.

1947-R No. 2
Clyfford Still

                  in hell's
       irruptive blaze
           & quivering heat
               & molten scarring
    a field of ox blood-
        colored fire
             ignites the mind's
    flammable surface &
        as it rips & tears
             as ragged flashes of black
    rise like the devil's
        tempting tongue
             there are trapped
    in this bottomless world
        in the parched
             center of this stifling life
    resilient splashes of white
        & so a little radiance
             breaks through
    the darkened heart

    how exhilarating
        its burst
             into consciousness
    & yet how far away
        from the burning soul
             its light

- IV -

Rag in Window
Alice Neel

After watching it
　　　year after year,
she nicknamed it
　　　the twentieth century.
In defense of despair
　　　that sad flag,
that tattered,
　　　unshamed thing
in bondage to one
　　　uncompromising nail
admits to nothing.
　　　Pillows of snow
and the twinned windowpanes
　　　and the dirt-brown building
are its witnesses.
　　　And then there's
the army-green,
　　　top-heavy cross
protecting
　　　those who live there:
a round-shouldered woman
　　　slicing onions into soup,
an Aztec-faced
　　　child or two
squealing as they chase
　　　imaginary bad guys
room to room.
　　　But what about the father?
Where is he?
　　　And what about

the easy chair
we don't see,
the one that's
empty that
he doesn't sit in at all?
Make up a life.
Your life.
Let it hang
off that city stone.
Let the torn thing blow.

Self-Portrait
Alice Bailly

I give you
half my face
    one eye gone
half my nose
    half
a lipsticked mouth
    and that drab
helmet of hair
    my shapeless torso
the paintbrush
    thinner than a cigarette
my elongated hands bland
    as old piano keys
only my palette
    boldly colored
and intense
    as the one good eye
zeroing in
    the way a raptor's will
the world splintering
    ten thousand ways
and crying out

Array IV
Sarah Walker

Return for the question
it's buried

restless patterns
the rhythm of interference

after gazing in the astonished waters
say *if only*

say *circle*
    light
        the skyline's glistening brow

down into the mineshaft of memory
back into the heartwell where

I hear there were mountains you walked
I hear there were lovers

it's incomparable
the way a life paces off
then accumulates

O blue bridge
O unseen bridge
O city of noise
O glass deep inside

Nocturne in Blue and Gold: Old Battersea Bridge
James Whistler

not so much a scene
as a mood
in those elusive city lights

reflected in water
the muted blue
chromatics of darkness

a twilight world
seen dimly as shapes dissolve
details disappear

not *a diet of fog*
as one critic complained
but a harbor

haunted
by golden rocket fire
cascading in evening air

by that old timber bridge
towering above the river
and the barge passing

underneath
carrying a lone figure
pushed up from the underworld

pure atmosphere
pulling me inside
where the formless world floats

On a Painting in *Onley's Arctic*

Out of sight of land
            for days…
Fog holds its breath,
            dims
A cloud-bank that appears
            carved from a glacier,
Blurs to the horizon
            a moving pattern of pack ice.

Out here, one welcomes variation.
One welcomes any area of rough relief:
    rubble field, pressure ridge,
        floe edges pushing up a steep-pitched roof.

Amid crawling islands of ice,
            flat water, a boat's quiet wood.

Sheer Curtains
Luc Tuymans

I do not know why I come to the window—
white curtains framed by a white wall.
The first breath of morning moves them.
They do not hesitate.
If rain dampens the leaded sill,
they shiver in the washed air,
waver when an animal heat crawls
hour by hour across the yard,
tremble when another summer
crumbles to dust. Some days
they refuse to move as if they hear
crows scolding them from the trees.
Soft as an owl's downy breast, they allow
the light of dawn into the house
to nest on the floor by the bed.
Behind them, everything fades.
I do not know why I come to the window.
A few flowers come up through the cloth,
petal by petal along a single branch of petals.
I do not know how long I have been here
looking through them but never drawing them aside.
What light there is shrinks on the curtains'
other side. I do not want to think of the world,
do not know where to put my gaze
when day falls into darkness
and the promise of sleep carries me away.

Red Vision

Leonor Fini

Someone took down the curtains

The furniture fell apart and disappeared

The clock stopped and the hours backed away

A misty figure listened at the window

How still and without a name it was

Around the corner red lit a fire

A phantom in flames floated off the floor

Said *Wake up now*

Said *Ask me what I want of you*

There in midair

Sickly and high-ceilinged

Imagine what the little wisp of a girl

Petal-white as a pond lily

The doorway loomed

The way the room began to tip

Her weightless hand hovered

As if a ghost in the presence of

The afterimage when you

Already it was too late to

Already it had gone too far

Nietzsche Contemplates Robert Ryman's *Courier II*

The real world accessible. World of white.
World as a painted aluminum sheet. Unframed.
The world for the moment. Inaccessible.
Pure, pearl-colored world. Unpromissable.
Fog of skepticism. Fog. Not acceded to.
Our world. Unknown. Not.
Not consolation. Not salvation.
First fog of reason. Obscured.
The real world refuted. Let's be rid of it.
I, Plato, am *the truth.* Ghostly spirit.
Ghostly anachronistic boy.
We have got rid of the real world.
What world is left?
What world?

Before the Caves
Helen Frankenthaler

before the bison appeared
the wild deer   before the hunter
arrived with the head of a bird
out of the cave   the steed of the gods
out of the rock-shelter
out of the grotto of the heart

back to a cleft in the earth
refuge/recess/prayer-niche

back to impetuous desire
it comes thundering

long before it was revered
before it sheltered demons and the dead

before the dead

before the allegory of
before the philosophers ruined it
when the world was darkness and night
Erebus and Nyx

then

and the moment after
when color exploded
flame red   ferric orange
the womb spewing
chlorine blue
sovereign purple
black as

Framed Sonogram

eyespot
    nose hole
        dimpled lip

the infolding embryo
    curls
        whitewalled

a little wave
    sets off across
        the surface of the face

a deepening crease
    repeated
        down through

navel
    anus
        urethra

that other face

this is how a body
    builds itself before
        it can breathe or see

cry or crouch
    before it coils into life
        twisting and heaving

as if locked in
    psychic battle
        with itself

but at this point
    with pain and intellection
        still separated

it is contortion
    without thought
        without a moment of distress

except for the mother
    who chose this plain
        metal frame

and a name

The road, the swallowing road
is flat; the sky, flat; the tedious,
autumnal field, the color range,
even the tonal variations, flat,
flat, flat. And the house—
the one without a path
leading to its dreary door,
without so much as a doorknob
to welcome you in? It's a box:
vernacular architecture,
the kind everybody understands.
And, inside? Perhaps a bed, a table,
two chairs, a working lantern.
Simple belongings without
a blessed soul in sight.
There's not even a passing sparrow
whistling the drab color of its song
or some lingering loosestrife
edging the roadside, but there is space.
A lot of it. Plenty to lose yourself in.
A hundred monotonous acres or more.
Bland landscapes offer few distractions—
a stand of weatherbeaten trees,
a few stars that ignite at night,
perhaps an occasional puff of wind
to escort a thought into oblivion.
With little more than dirt
for company, what is timeless
hangs between ground and sky.
The body retreats from a place

where every breath is a monument
to what isn't there, and nowhere
is everywhere, wherever you look.

Autumn Rhythm
Jackson Pollock

bark-colored scythe marks
    oily black splashes
        sinews of cinder gray

the debris of a season

threads of quiet colors
    crammed together
        against the thinning days

⟎

the first blizzard
    flies through
        kicking up
little heaps of color
    until everything is blurred
        by swirling snow

in the wilderness of the painter's head
a sudden squall of longing

⟎

root-crawl
    choreographed hooks
        and loops and commas
drippings that set up
    a rhythm that

undulates across the canvas
as if the paint itself
has learned to dance

☙

in the illumined air
a leaf's sharp tip
arrows down in the dirt—
a perfect shot—

as an expansive thought
twirls away from words
curls away

from the withered crops
that rot after frost
from the ground that
smells like a grave

☙

an insect's last
exuberant courtship dance
before the season ends

...but the effect is calming
despite the
sticks
and trowels

and knives
   that make up a life
the raw autumn wind
   flung
      into the face of things

The Uncertainty of the Poet

Giorgio de Chirico

Near the dark arches of the arcade,
a headless, plaster torso of a woman.
By her dimpled hip, two dozen
green and yellow bruised bananas.

Off in the distance,
a train with its ample banner of steam
speeds left into oblivion. Menacing,
monumental shadows master what we see.
Wait: the wish of reason is reversed.
The poet aims her words at what's unworded,
startled by the horizon's vaporous wall.

Untitled (Mélisande)
Joseph Cornell

In the collage of the imagination,
The requirement of skin is dismissed.
A plastic face can be animate.

[Constructed wall of beach debris,
Rough wall with a window cut out.
Doomed doll at the window
Practicing her little I of privacy.]

The mind watches itself watching.

Shipwreck of loneliness.
Sand-packed prison
Shutting in, shutting out.

Dreaming of Picasso

All night an accelerating
geometry of eyes—hundreds
shaped like birds or boats
or beetles, simplified to dots
or crosses or a pair of 2s or mis-
matched diamonds, perfect zeros,
scoops of moon placed sidewise
or lengthwise on a face, slipping
out of orbit on a cheek, hung
under an ear, planted mid-forehead,
paper-thin planes of them,
each one alive and staring
from the dislocated faces of wives,
lovers, mothers, serene and lopsided,
splintered, wrenching, ravaged,
a proliferating gallery of women,
terraced in my head as I sleep,
and my own curious eye:
steering toward what it perceives,
capturing exact duplicates of each
stylized eye I run by,
as I race to comprehend
what I'm taking in, what expression
I'd see if I raised the mirror
to find my own eye, distorted
and floating above an iron cheek.

Thought
Auguste Rodin

Her head issuing
out of roughly-hewn marble
has no body—simply that head
in earthbound union with stone.

No restless energy to express.
No file marks, no sign of a chisel,
none of the gouging, chipping, dusting,
that must have occupied Rodin's mind.

Her polished face, smoother and glossier
than skin could ever be,
does not focus on envy or despair
but on something epistemological:

How, I can almost hear her say,
do we come to know the world?

And in that musing, such simplicity of form:
in the slight tension above her eyes,
in the shadow of her mouth,
under the arches of her brow.

Like a novitiate
crowned as she is by that modest cap,
she has what Lamartine once said of Balzac:
the face of an element.

Chin still half-sunk in the stone
from which she rose,
she is inseparable from the source
and so, at peace, serene in contemplation.

How do we come to know the world?
Not only with feet and fingers but
with down-tilted head gazing at then past
the surface from which everything ascends.

In her cumulating thought
only that flawless lucidity: spirit made
manifest in the sweep of the lines,
the contours of her cheeks,
her glorious forehead graced with light.

Untitled (rear view of nude)
Man Ray

Neither the lascivious rump of a monkey
nor the flashy buttocks of a baboon.
No suggestion of the crimson vulva,
the showy, red-lipped rear.
No hint of a bald, fringed anus
erupting like a boil or a soft piece of fruit.
No licentious distraction here. No
sexual signaling in this chaste,
inverted heart, this pear-shaped
derrière. In the erotic
S of the body, her flesh is idle,
tranquil as a pillow. Her thoughts
are elsewhere. Given such nonchalance,
who cares about the relationship
between plane and protuberance?
Naked man is a mollusc, Lacan wrote,
but he never saw this milkwhite bottom,
this silken pair of thighs.
There's grace in her well-rounded flesh
as if, as Apollinaire once said,
an angel had puffed out its cheeks.
This is an adored, triumphant,
spiritualized backside. Not so much
a body part as a potent, untouchable idea.
The vertical cleft separating the buttocks,
two ample, harmonious halves, becomes
a bridge. One takes comfort in this
opulent bottom which does not bother—
like hands or lips or eyes—with emotion
but simply expresses its tender presence

as if it were a cloud or a shell or a scroll.
I am the celestial sphere. *I* am divinity
expressed in the exquisite curves of the world.